Focus on Climate Change

CLIMATE CHANGE BASICS

What Is Happening to Our World

KAYLA ANDRA

TWENTY-FIRST CENTURY BOOKS / MINNEAPOLIS

For Alan, Andre, Anthony, Erica, Cash, and Paige.

Twenty-First Century Books™
An imprint of Lerner Publishing Group, Inc.
241 First Avenue North
Minneapolis, MN 55401 USA

For reading levels and more information, look up this title at www.lernerbooks.com.

Main body text set in Bembo Std Regular.
Typeface provided by Monotype Typography.

Library of Congress Cataloging-in-Publication Data

Names: Andra, Kayla, author.
Title: Climate change basics : what is happening to our world / Kayla Andra.
Description: Minneapolis : Twenty-First Century Books , 2026. | Series: Focus on climate change | Includes bibliographical references and index. | Audience: Ages 11–18 | Audience: Grades 7–9 | Summary: "Discover how human activity began harming the environment, starting with the Industrial Revolution. Then learn how modern actions exacerbate this harm. This scientific breakdown of climate change explains the planet's energy balance and much more"—Provided by publisher.
Identifiers: LCCN 2025011145 (print) | LCCN 2025011146 (ebook) | ISBN 9798765644232 (library binding) | ISBN 9798348029609 (paperback) | ISBN 9798348000189 (epub)
Subjects: LCSH: Climatic changes—Juvenile literature | Climatic changes—Effect of human beings on—Juvenile literature | LCGFT: Literature
Classification: LCC QC981.8.C5 A53 2026 (print) | LCC QC981.8.C5 (ebook) | DDC 304.2/8—dc23/eng/20250716

LC record available at https://lccn.loc.gov/2025011145
LC ebook record available at https://lccn.loc.gov/2025011146

Manufactured in the United States of America
1-1012705-52449-5/2/2025

CONTENTS

INTRODUCTION

In 2023 a series of uncontrollable and deadly wildfires ignited and burned throughout Canada. These record-breaking fires resulted in billions of dollars of damage and caused hundreds of thousands of people to flee from their homes to save their lives. In addition to the devastating damage done to much of Canada's land and many of its citizens, other countries also felt the impact of these megafires. The smoke from the fires reached as far as China and some countries in Europe, polluting the air and worsening the air quality for many people.

Disasters and wildfires such as the ones in 2023 in Canada are increasing in frequency and severity because of climate change. Projections of possible future impacts indicate that such disasters and effects are likely to get worse.

Families, such as the Carlson family of the Halifax, Nova Scotia, area, reported feelings of deep sorrow. Brianne Carlson, her husband, and her two-year-old were evacuated from their home as one of the raging 2023 wildfires charged toward them. She and her family escaped just as the embers

Four months of raging wildfires across Canada in the summer of 2023 had widespread effects, reducing air quality in northern US cities such as New York.

were crackling up her driveway, burning in their minds the last memory they would have of their home. Due to megafires caused by climate change, many families such as the Carlson family were forced to relocate and start new lives.

These kinds of events are just the tip of the iceberg when it comes to climate change threats. While coastal communities worldwide struggle with rising sea levels and needing to relocate, fishers face difficulty catching enough fish to eat, feed their communities, or make a livable wage due to coral bleaching and declining fish populations. Farmers face shifting seasons that disrupt their farming routines and growing patterns, reducing the amount of food they can harvest. From record-high summer temperatures to devastating winter storms, extreme weather patterns are increasing alongside natural disasters. These are not isolated issues. Everyone around the world is facing the consequences of climate change.

Climate Change

What comes to mind when you hear the term *climate change*? You may think of a firsthand experience. If not, perhaps dramatic headlines flash through your mind. Maybe you heard or read about the most expensive climate change event in history, Hurricane Ian, which caused an estimated $113 billion in damage in 2021. You have likely encountered other news stories focusing on record-breaking temperatures, destructive wildfires, and unusual catastrophes. You might imagine melting glaciers, troubled polar bears, bleached-white coral reefs, and declining sea life populations. With so many different consequences, the topic of climate change can become overwhelming. How are the impacts so diverse? What exactly is climate change?

The United Nations Framework Convention on Climate Change (UNFCCC) defines climate change as "a change of climate which is attributed directly or indirectly to human activity that alters the composition of the global atmosphere and which is in addition to natural climate variability observed over comparable periods." Let's break this down. First the UNFCCC mentions humanity's

When they think of climate change, many people think of scenes such as polar bears getting stranded as their habitat melts around them.

role in climate change. Humans are, purposefully or not, causing these changes. The definition also mentions both time and long-term change. Climate change does not refer to day-to-day changes in our weather patterns. Instead, climate change involves long-term and permanent changes in weather and climate. Examples include the rising number of cyclones in the Pacific and global temperatures increasing over several years. The UNFCCC also mentions the term *climate variability*. The difference between climate change and climate variability is the cause of change. Climate variability is the natural changes in climate over long periods. Climate variability explains why Earth has naturally shifted from ice ages to volcanic periods, even before humans ever walked Earth. On the other hand, climate change is not natural.

It is also important to understand that climate change and global warming are not the same thing, though they are related, and both are caused by humans. Global warming only refers to the rise in Earth's surface temperature over a long period. It is only one part of climate change.

Climate change has major consequences for all living beings. For people, it affects us socially, costs us financially, and threatens our homes and food supply. It also threatens wildlife, altering and damaging their ecosystems. But how does climate change happen? How long has it been going on? And what can be done about it?

CHAPTER ONE

Climate, Weather, and Climate Change

Climate and weather impact our daily lives. They impact small things, such as what clothes we wear each day. But they also affect our food, health, water quality, and even our moods. It is well known that the weather influences mental health. Sunlight is like nature's medicine for better moods and lower rates of depression. Studies have found that weather may even shape personalities. Warmer weather tends to create more extroverted people. This is likely because warmer weather boosts vitamin D levels and encourages people to go outside and have more encounters with others. Weather also impacts our physical health. For example, changes in weather and atmospheric pressure affect blood pressure and how efficiently our hearts pump blood through our bodies. Changes in air pressure can spark pain in muscles and joints or cause sinus pressure.

It's easy to see how weather and climate are important in our lives, but what is the difference between weather and climate? Also, what is climate change?

Gathering to enjoy the sunshine is a popular activity, especially in places that have limited amounts of sunny weather.

Weather vs. Climate

American author Mark Twain made famous a late-1800s saying about how to think of the difference between weather and climate: "Climate is what you expect, while weather is what you get." Both climate and weather include factors such as precipitation, wind, humidity, and sunshine. So, what is the main difference between weather and climate? Weather is short-term, with small events and transitions that can occur in one day or even a few minutes. For example, a cool morning might turn into a warm afternoon and then change again into a windy evening. The climate is the average long-term conditions in a specific region.

People often talk about a place and its climate by discussing the typical seasonal changes and temperatures expected throughout the year.

To understand climate, imagine that you live along the coastline of Southern California. It is mid-June, and when you walk out of your front door, you probably expect to squint your eyes due to the bright sun and experience warm temperatures of about 75°F (24°C). However, when you walk outside, you are surprised to see cloudy skies and feel a frigid breeze. Where do climate and weather fit in this situation? The climate would be the warmth you expect because warm temperatures are the norm for your region at this time of the year. The weather would be the unusually cool breeze you experience instead.

How does climate change fit into this? Imagine that your warm California summers start to turn colder and colder so that over the next thirty years, you gradually begin to consider it normal to wear sweaters in June. This would be an example of climate change because your average summer temperatures and weather patterns have permanently changed over a long period.

What Determines Climate?

Now that you know the difference between weather and climate, what are the factors that make up the climate? Many elements influence the climate that you live in and experience. The two most important elements are precipitation and temperature, which are both influenced by other factors as well. Some of these factors are latitude, altitude, and the Coriolis effect.

Existing as far away from the equator as possible, Antarctica is one of the coldest and driest places on Earth.

When we talk about latitude, we are talking about a region's location and distance from the equator. Locations closer to the equator have more tropical climates with higher humidity and warmer temperatures. Locations far north or south of the equator, such as Antarctica, experience frostier conditions, drier air, and permanent glaciers. An area's altitude (distance above sea level) also affects its climate. As altitude increases, the air becomes thinner, and the air in the atmosphere absorbs less direct sun at high altitudes, causing temperatures to drop.

The Coriolis effect plays a significant role in the development of cyclones, weather systems, wind patterns, ocean currents, and temperature. The Coriolis effect is a phenomenon that occurs in rotating systems on Earth. Since our planet rotates on an axis, any moving mass or gust of wind (including objects and ocean currents) experiences a force that causes it to deflect, or curve away, from its original

Current Conditions

Another important part of Earth's climate is ocean currents. Both the wind and the Coriolis effect help determine ocean currents and cause two processes: Ekman transport and the Ekman spiral. Ekman transport is when the wind blows across the sea, moving the water on the ocean's surface. Due to the Coriolis effect, when the wind moves the water, it swirls at an angle (to the right in the northern hemisphere and the left in the southern hemisphere). As the ocean depth changes, the swirling turns into spiraling. This spiraling motion is called the Ekman spiral, and these spirals create ocean currents. As climate change occurs and wind patterns permanently change, so will processes such as Ekman transport and the Ekman spiral. This is one way climate change impacts ocean currents and can change entire ocean ecosystems that have adapted to or are dependent on a particular current.

direction. This means that moving objects and even air swirl to the right (making clockwise rotations) in the northern hemisphere and curve to the left (making counterclockwise rotations) in the southern hemisphere.

To understand the Coriolis effect, imagine that you and a friend want to throw a ball back and forth from the equator to the north pole. Even if you throw the ball in a straight line to where your friend is standing, the ball will appear to them as though it is curving and land somewhere else. This is because Earth is rotating beneath the ball's path. Pilots must consider the Coriolis effect when they are planning flights because it affects wind, all objects in the sky, and the airplane's route.

CHAPTER TWO

The Sun and Climate Change

The sun supplies all the energy required to support life on Earth. It gives plants life by supporting photosynthesis. The sun drives the planet's water cycle and, most importantly, keeps it habitable. It also contributes to Earth's climate. Even small changes in Earth's relationship to the sun can change life as we know it. For example, paleoclimatologists (scientists who study historic climates) have found that previous slight changes in Earth's orbit around the sun are linked to historic ice ages, glacial periods, and other dramatic climate shifts. So, if the sun plays such an important role in temperature and climate, could it have something to do with climate change? To answer this question, we must understand Earth's energy balance and how the sun's energy transfers to our planet.

Earth's Energy Balance

Earth's energy balance is the exchange of the energies that enter and leave our atmosphere. The sun's energy either remains trapped in the air of our atmosphere, is absorbed into Earth's surface, or is reflected into space. Of all the energy that enters our atmosphere, only about 70 percent hits the ground and is absorbed by Earth's surface. The other 30 percent is either reflected into space by clouds, snow, and ice or remains in the atmosphere for some time, influencing our climate.

The incoming and outgoing energy should be equal. Otherwise, it will be out of balance, and climate change can occur. If there is too much incoming solar energy without the same amount of outgoing energy, the climate will warm. Similarly, if there is too much outgoing energy and not enough incoming solar energy, the climate will cool. So, it is important to monitor the transfer of energy so that we can sustain its delicate balance and prevent climate change. One thing we can monitor to maintain the balance is the things that reflect energy to space, including snow, ice, and clouds. Scientists monitor these things by measuring albedo.

Albedo

Albedo refers to the amount of energy an object can either absorb or reflect. Different objects, environments, and parts of Earth's surface interact differently with the sun's energy. This gives them each a different albedo. Objects or surfaces that are dark in color and reflect little energy have a low albedo. Objects or surfaces that are light-colored and reflect a lot of energy have a high albedo. For example, clouds, ice, and snow-covered surfaces have high reflectivity and high albedo, while oceans and forests have low reflectivity and low albedo. Albedo allows climate scientists to measure the

Don't Blame the Sun

In the past, people debated the role of the sun in climate change. Some thought that the sun played a bigger part in climate change than it does. To help settle the debate, scientists developed unique climate models. Climate models are computer programs that make predictions based on factors that affect climate (such as wind, precipitation, latitude, longitude, and albedo). The new models use more data and consider more climate factors to understand how the sun contributes to climate change. Based on the results, most scientists conclude that the sun does not play a big role in climate change. Instead, human activity is to blame. Data applied to these models largely supports this perspective since the rates of climate change since the 1970s are too rapid to be caused by orbital changes and too extreme to be the result of solar energy shifts.

Scientists use climate data to run models that help them understand how different factors contribute to climate change.

planet's incoming and outgoing energy, which is fundamental for studying climate change. If Earth's temperatures rise and cause ice to melt rapidly, then there will be fewer reflective surfaces and less energy reflected into space. This causes more energy to be absorbed, warming Earth's surface further and melting even more ice. This result is known as ice-albedo feedback. It demonstrates how a tiny change in Earth's energy balance can speed up climate change.

Earth's Energy Balance and Climate Change

How do the sun, Earth's energy balance, and albedo contribute to climate change? Although the sun affects Earth's climate and keeps our planet warm, ultimately it is not responsible for the alarming rate of climate change.

As for Earth's energy balance, climate change happens when this balance is disrupted. For example, if an imbalance occurs because energy is being trapped in our atmosphere, Earth can heat up. This affects albedo, amplifies the ice-albedo feedback loop, and turns up the warming effect.

We see this in the twenty-first century. Our energy system is out of balance due to increasing heat-trapping human activities. Research from the National Aeronautics and Space Administration (NASA) and the National Oceanic and Atmospheric Administration (NOAA) found that between 2005 and 2019, the imbalance in Earth's energy balance system doubled, meaning that Earth was trapping more and more energy. Similar findings in the Intergovernmental Panel on Climate Change (IPCC) 2021 reports show that even more energy is being absorbed by the planet than reflected, demonstrating that this trend continues. But, like climate change overall, this ongoing imbalance is not because of the sun. Human activity, which we'll discuss more in chapter four, causes the imbalance.

Carbon-emitting human activity is primarily responsible for the sharp rise in Earth's energy imbalance in the twenty-first century.

CHAPTER THREE

The Long History of Climate Change

Since Earth formed about 4.5 billion years ago, it has experienced dramatic climate transformations. It has gone from having glacial ice ages to hot periods when oceans were an estimated 176°F (80°C) to the milder, varying temperatures modern life experiences. These natural changes in Earth's climate are known as natural variability.

Paleoclimatology

Earth's climate naturally changes over time because of long-term factors, such as Earth's orbit and distance from the sun. There are also short-term factors, such as volcanic eruptions or abrupt changes in ocean currents. The combination of these elements causing noticeable changes takes thousands of years.

If Earth's climate naturally changes, how do we know that climate change is not part of its natural climate cycle? The answer is in studying and understanding Earth's ancient climates. Paleoclimatologists aim to determine

Volcanic eruptions, such as this one at Mauna Loa in Hawai'i from 2022, can affect Earth's climate in the short term.

"normal" rates of climate change and to understand the past better. This helps show how much humans are impacting the climate.

Historic Climate Records

Satellite and instrumental data help paleoclimatologists study climate. In 1654 the first usable thermometer instrument was invented. It was only in the late eighteenth century, about 100 years later, that people started consistent and long-term temperature records. As technology advanced, scientists developed more instruments to measure temperature, humidity, and other climate factors. Some of the instruments include space-bound satellites, buoys, aircraft, and space stations. But these advancements only give scientists the ability to study climate conditions from the past 150 years. How do they study even older climates?

Paleoclimatologists study natural elements that give clues to what Earth's climate looked like in the past. These clues are called proxy records and include tree rings, pollen remains, fossils, and living organisms. For example, trees form rings each year during their growing season as they produce cambium (new wood) layers under the bark. The new wood contains climate evidence and is a natural record of that year's conditions. A thicker tree ring indicates a warmer, more humid, and rainier year. A thinner ring means a drier and colder year. Likewise, polar ice sheets and ice cores have tiny, conserved bubbles of air from the ancient

In many parts of the world, tree rings can provide a climate history for hundreds of years. Scientists can compare older rings to newer rings to help understand how the climate has changed.

atmosphere. These little bubbles of atmosphere are perfect mirrors of past rainfall and temperature data.

Thanks to proxy data, scientists have a clear understanding of ancient climate. They have discovered that ice completely covered Earth during the Cryogenian Period (about 720 million to 635 million years ago). They found that this "snowball Earth" phase was when life formed in the seas and was the likely source of humans' ancient ancestors. During the Eocene Epoch (66 million to 23 million years ago), the entire globe had a tropical climate, with no ice cap to be found. Between those two periods, about 100 million years ago, dinosaurs roamed Earth, enjoying the hotter climates and lush tropical environments. Our planet has had many other landscapes and climate cycles, supporting life forms we may never have imagined. But unlike the changing climates of Earth's past, modern rates of climate change are not natural.

Natural vs. Unnatural Climate Change

As paleoclimatology technologies advanced and more people suffered climate change impacts, two things became clear: climate change is occurring, and human activity is the cause. For example, in 1988 James Hansen, a researcher working with NASA, released a report showing that the planet was getting warmer. Hansen testified in the Senate later that year, definitively naming human activity as the cause for rising temperatures. He also warned of increasing severe weather events. In response, the United Nations created the IPCC to examine the evidence and determine how much humanity was contributing to climate change. It took until 1995, but

Record-Breaking Evidence

When NASA sounded the alarm in 1988, the global average temperature was hovering around 1.1°F (0.6°C), above temperature averages from before the Industrial Revolution (1733–1913). Since then weather stations around the world have reported that daily heat temperature records have been broken more than 2.3 million times. And 2023 was the warmest year on record, with future years expected to keep breaking the record. That year's global average temperatures were around 2.65°F (1.45°C) above the pre-industrial average baseline (56.7°F (13.7°C)), making the past decade the hottest ever recorded.

Thousands of weather stations around the world are used to determine that the planet's average temperature continues to increase.

the IPCC decided they had enough evidence to confidently confirm the Hansen and NASA findings that human activity was responsible for the increasing rates of climate change. As a result, climate change became a hotly debated political issue.

One reason for the public's polarized opinion was the climate change countermovement funded by big oil companies. Countermovement organizations aim to spread misinformation and raise uncertainty about climate change to protect the huge profits made by running operations that are causing the crisis. In other words, since burning oil and gas is the main reason that the atmosphere is getting warmer, there was a financial and corporate motive for oil companies to spread misinformation about climate change. Since 1988 almost three-quarters of all harmful emissions have come from just one hundred fossil fuel producers. Just 23 out of 195 countries are responsible for most of these emissions.

Illustrating how much these companies invested in spreading misinformation, one report found that one oil company alone spent more than $16 million on campaigns to confuse the public about human activity, fossil fuels, and climate change. These campaigns not only succeeded in spreading misinformation and confusing the public, but they also caused a major delay in global action.

Regardless of the confusion, the fact that humans are the main cause of climate change is undeniable. With time, more people began to see past the misinformation and accept this truth. The annual IPCC reports also continued to prove the campaigns wrong. In 2001 the IPCC claimed that it was 66 percent probable that human activities were the main culprit of recent warming trends. Then in the 2007 reports, the probability increased to 90 percent. Adding to the IPCC

Fossil fuel companies have used large sums from their record profits to fuel misinformation about their products.

reports, Hansen's predictions of global warming and climate change impacts began coming true, from extended droughts and raging wildfires to catastrophic hurricanes and rising sea levels. By 2020 more than 99 percent of the scientific community agreed that climate change was a human-caused issue that demands global-scale action. But how do humans impact climate change?

CHAPTER FOUR

Human Activity and Climate Change

Modern humans have existed for more than two hundred thousand years, and human-caused climate change started about one hundred years ago. So, human presence alone, apart from human activity, may not be the cause. When did human activity become a problem? It all started with the Industrial Revolutions.

The First Industrial Revolution

Historians say there were not just one but four industrial revolutions. The Industrial Revolutions represent a worldwide transition in the speed and efficiency of making goods using advancing technologies. They mark the start of modern society and the transition from creation by hand to dependency on machines and technology. In just a few decades, horse-pulled wagons were swapped for automobiles. Electric light and kitchen appliances replaced fire. Small farms turned into large-scale agricultural operations. In general, machinery replaced humans and animals (such as horses, mules, and oxen) to complete many small and exhausting tasks. This is industrialization.

The First Industrial Revolution started in Great Britain. James Hargreaves invented one of the first major innovations,

The invention of the spinning jenny is credited as one of the launching events of the First Industrial Revolution.

the spinning jenny, in about 1760 to turn cotton and wool into material. The spinning jenny had eight spindles that were powered by one wheel and one person, producing materials faster than ever before.

This invention started a new kind of work in factories, mills, and large-scale production. Day-to-day life transitioned from multitasking and farm work to single factory tasks, with workers doing the same job every day. Families moved from small towns and farms to urban areas since factories were built in and around cities. This resulted in mass urbanization. Villages expanded into bustling towns, and towns transformed into more modern cities. These trends spread throughout Europe, trickled over to the United States in the 1790s, and advanced throughout the rest of the globe. Together, urbanization and industrialization meant large-scale, carbon-emitting machines that negatively impacted the environment almost wholly replaced human activities that had low carbon impact.

One of the biggest negative environmental impacts of the first revolution was how it changed food production. Small family farms turned into large-scale, single-crop (monocrop) producers. Single-crop farms damage soil quality and fertility because the plants continuously absorb the same nutrients, disrupting the soil nutrient balance. The soil relies on a variety of plants and animals living in the ecosystems to rejuvenate, making the land less usable over time. Monocrop production also caused chemical pollution since farmers introduced lots of new herbicides and pesticides. Plus, deforestation skyrocketed around this time. People cleared trees and natural areas to make way for large-scale factories, cities, and growing populations. About 160 years after the first revolution, researchers estimated that more than 34 percent of all fertile soil on Earth had declined in quality. Between the increase in pollution in cities and the worsening of natural ecosystems, climate change quickly grew into a global environmental crisis.

The Revolution Evolves

For all the new machinery and factories, the first revolution relied on coal and metals to build and power steam engines.

The rate of deforestation across the United States increased sharply in the 1800s.

The second revolution followed, peaking around 1870, and revolved around the use of gas, oil, and electricity. Around the same time, cars and planes were invented, which sparked a new and booming transportation industry that carried its own environmental impacts. By 1913 Henry Ford revolutionized production by creating the assembly line in his car factory. The process helped create more products at a quicker pace in several industries, which also contributed to more consumption of goods, more waste, and more pollution. The first and second revolutions are the two that most people are talking about when they discuss the Industrial Revolutions. But two more revolutions followed.

The third revolution, also known as the Information Age, began in the 1970s, powered by the emergence of electronics and nuclear energy. This emergence came at a cost. For example, advanced technologies such as smartphones are made of rare minerals that require drilling into the earth and destroying the surrounding environment to extract. From sourcing to building to throwing away electronics, each phase damages the environment and emits high amounts of chemical pollution. Electronic waste is also the fastest-growing type of waste in the world. Finally, the fourth revolution started in 2000. The fourth revolution is all about the shift to renewable energy sources and artificial intelligence.

In many ways, the Industrial Revolutions changed life on Earth. People have advanced in agriculture, food production, health care, pharmaceuticals, and transportation. In the last few hundred years, we have invented microwaves, smartphones and smarter computers, airplanes and automobiles, refrigeration and air conditioning, the Internet, and more. But with each revolution and each invention comes an environmental

The Potential of the Fourth Revolution

The ongoing fourth revolution has many promising advantages. Rapid advancements in technology such as the Internet and smartphones have connected the entire world by making global communication effortless. The Internet of Things (a network of devices and objects that have software and online network connectivity) and artificial intelligence (AI) dominate how we communicate and plan for the future. Advancements are also occurring in energy-conserving technologies. These technologies have the potential to help lessen climate change impacts. Thanks to AI, algorithms that analyze and suggest improvements for new technologies and renewable energy technologies such as water, wind, and solar systems are increasing in efficiency and becoming more affordable. Scientists claim that the fourth revolution is rapidly increasing the use of renewable energy sources, likely because of the increased accessibility. Therefore, the fourth revolution could be the first revolution to help decrease rather than increase the impacts of climate change.

Rapid advances in technology have made wind and solar energy collection affordable and efficient.

footprint. For example, advanced transportation systems come with a rise in pollution and climate change. This is especially true in the United States, where transportation is responsible for almost one-third of harmful carbon emissions.

Additionally, along with these innovations came a massive increase in consumer culture and the use of consumer goods in certain parts of the industrialized world. Consumer culture describes a modern society where many citizens are hyper-focused on the use of material goods and where waste production is higher than ever. To meet the rising population's increasing demand for goods, matched equally by the corporate demand for profits, many corporations make items as cheaply and efficiently as possible.

But cheap production rarely considers sustainability and is prioritized over helping or protecting the environment. For example, take plastic production, usage, and waste. Plastic is a versatile, durable, and cheap material that has enhanced our lives, from its contribution to the medical industry to its presence in our day-to-day routines. But together, people produce more than 450 tons (408 t) of plastic every year while properly recycling only a small fraction of it. This has caused a destructive waste problem, affecting wildlife ecosystems and polluting our water and food systems with microplastics. On top of the waste, the production of cheap materials such as plastic also contributes to climate change since they are made from fossil fuels.

Fossil Fuels

As the centuries have progressed, countries experiencing the fourth revolution have reached a point where enormous amounts of energy are spent on transportation, power generation, food production, and the production of goods in general. Where does the energy to support the massive spike in demand for material products come from? Fossil fuels, including oil, coal, and gas, supply most of the world's energy demands. But fossil fuels are nonrenewable, meaning their supply is limited, and their reserves will eventually run out. This means that dependency on these resources is not sustainable.

Most of the world's energy needs are met by consuming fossil fuels, an unsustainable method.

Adding to the limited supply, the entire process of harvesting and using fossil fuels damages Earth's environment and climate. Extracting fossil fuels directly destroys the environment. Most fossil fuels are found below Earth's surface, which requires mining or drilling for access. In addition to physically damaging the environment, drilling and mining for fossil fuels contribute to rising temperatures and climate change in multiple ways. One study found that increasing temperatures and rates of climate change were sometimes six times higher in regions where fossil fuels are extracted. This is because the land surface plays an important role in regulating temperatures.

For example, let's take a closer look at the petroleum industry. Petroleum is also known as crude oil or gasoline, and its production is one of the main culprits of climate change. For crude oil to be extracted from the ocean floor, a destructive drilling process is necessary to access the seabound oil reserves. Before drilling begins, scientists perform seismic surveys to search the sea for worthwhile oil reserves. The surveys alone threaten wildlife, causing sound pollution that disrupts animal communication, mating, and migration. Once the drilling spot is determined, oil platforms are created, and oil rigs are shipped in, occasionally causing toxic oil spills. After the oil is extracted, it must be burned and refined, releasing tons of carbon dioxide into our atmosphere. The IPCC approximates that the oil industry alone is responsible for one-third of the world's carbon emissions.

CHAPTER FIVE

Greenhouse Gases 101

Not only does the extraction of fossil fuels harm the environment, but so do the toxic gases that fossil fuels emit when burned. These toxic gases are called greenhouse gases. Since the beginning of the Industrial Revolutions, greenhouse gas emissions have escalated, almost tripling between the 1970s and 2020s alone. Innovation occurred so fast that people did not know about the negative consequences of burning greenhouse gases at first. But from England's Guy Callendar in the 1930s to American Dr. John Mercer in the 1960s, scientists have been blaming carbon emissions for rising temperatures for decades. Those claims were mostly ignored until the 1980s, when scientists linked greenhouse gas emissions to the deterioration of the ozone layer and the withering of the atmosphere.

Greenhouse Gases and Chemistry

The main greenhouse gases include carbon dioxide, nitrous oxide, methane, and chlorofluorocarbons (CFCs), also called

Aerosol sprays contain human-made fluorinated gases, which are harmful due to high potency.

fluorinated gases. Each gas has different chemical properties. When gases are emitted, they stay in the atmosphere for different amounts of time. Some even stay there indefinitely. The amount of time a gas remains in the atmosphere is called its lifetime. Each gas also has a different potency, which is the measurement of how effectively the gas traps heat in the atmosphere.

Fluorinated gases, also known as industrial gases, are human made. These are the only greenhouse gases that do not naturally occur in our atmosphere. These synthetic gases are used to manufacture goods, added into aerosol cans, and for refrigeration. Fluorinated gases only comprise 3 percent of all greenhouse gas emissions. Yet their high potencies and lifetimes make them a major threat. Compared to carbon dioxide, fluorinated gases are thousands of times more potent and have longer lifetimes. They are more effective at trapping heat and can stay in our atmosphere for thousands of years.

Methane and nitrous oxide are two other gases that have small emissions but high potency. Nitrous oxide (a gas emitted from agricultural machinery and burning fossil fuels) is almost three hundred times more potent than carbon dioxide. It also stays in the atmosphere for more than one hundred years, even though it only makes up 6 percent of emissions. Methane is a by-product of natural gas extraction and transportation. It accounts for about 12 percent of emissions but is almost one hundred times more potent than carbon dioxide and has a lifetime of about twelve years.

What do all these gases have to do with carbon dioxide? Carbon dioxide (CO_2) is the biggest contributor to global warming and climate change. It can stay in our atmosphere for up to one thousand years. Carbon dioxide accounts for almost 80 percent of emissions and is released when fossil fuels are burned, including driving and flying, which accounts for nearly 35 percent of CO_2 emissions. Electricity production accounts for another 31 percent of carbon dioxide emissions. Cement production and other

Carbon dioxide makes up nearly 80 percent of all greenhouse gas emissions.

Learning to Monitor Greenhouse Gases

For information about the gases in the atmosphere, NASA is a great resource. It provides free online resources that show what it is like to be a climate scientist who works with greenhouse gases. NASA's greenhouse data pathfinder demonstrates how to access their remote sensing data. The remote sensing data reveals what greenhouse gases are in the atmosphere and how much of them are in each region. NASA also provides free access to its Carbon Mapper, a resource that helps pinpoint and view major emission spots from space.

NASA uses satellites to gather information on major greenhouse gas emission locations on the surface of Earth.

industrial processes are also big CO_2 emitters. Deforestation also contributes because trees store carbon in their leaves, stems, trunks, roots, and surrounding soil. Therefore, when people cut down trees to clear land, the trees release CO_2. Plus, fewer trees mean fewer places for excess carbon to go. In short, carbon dioxide is the star (or main villain) of the fossil fuel contribution to climate change.

Greenhouse Gases and Humanity

Greenhouse gas emissions are harmful to human health. Industrial processes (such as burning fuel, producing electricity, and manufacturing goods) release pollutants and toxins into the air humans breathe. Carbon dioxide emissions alone are linked to a decrease in overall human health and lifespan. This is because increasing amounts of carbon dioxide in the air furthers the risk of respiratory and heart diseases. Some studies have noted elevated chances of premature death with more carbon dioxide in the atmosphere. Greenhouse gas emissions continue to rise, and their effects extend beyond environmental damage and human health risks. Animals and other wildlife all face the same or similar threats. Due to the greenhouse effect, these emissions are also the main cause of the climate change crisis.

The Greenhouse Effect

The greenhouse effect got its name because it causes the atmosphere to behave similarly to a greenhouse. The glass roof and walls of a greenhouse allow sunlight to shine through, providing warmth for plants to thrive. While sunlight and warmth can come in, the glass does not allow heat to escape, trapping it and raising the temperature inside the greenhouse. Greenhouse gases work similarly, as they allow sunlight to come into our atmosphere, trap it, and raise the temperature of Earth's surface. The increased concentration of greenhouse gases results in a thick "blanket" of gases over our atmosphere, trapping in more and more heat. As a result, it disrupts Earth's energy balance and causes climate change.

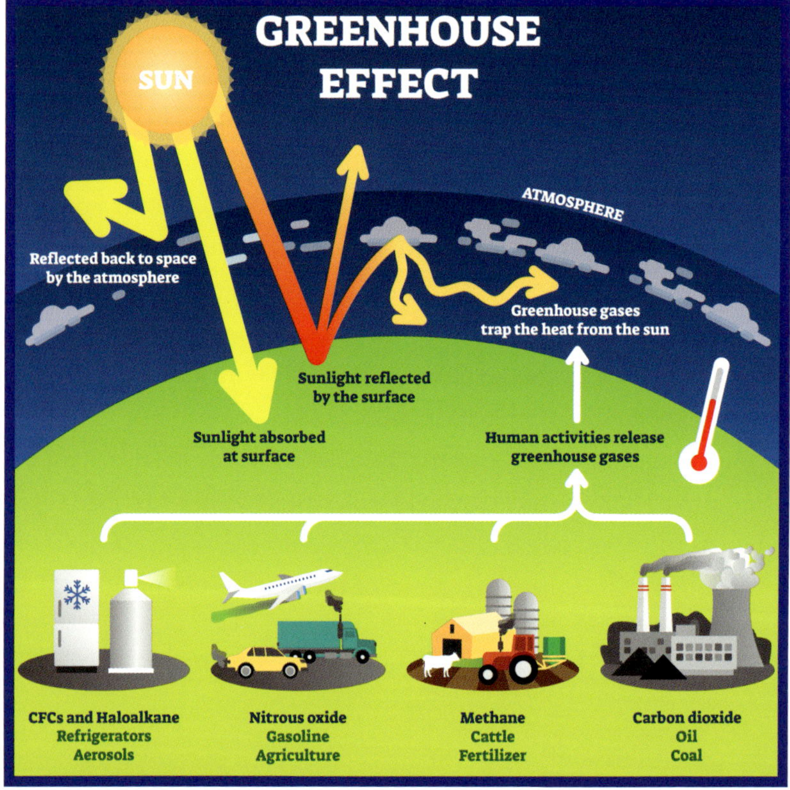

Greenhouse gases, mainly caused by human activity, form a layer in the atmosphere that traps heat. This is known as the greenhouse effect.

CHAPTER SIX

Impacts on Our Planet

Now we know a bit about the history, causes, chemistry, and some impacts of climate change. What are the rest of the consequences? What will be the future impacts of global warming and climate change?

Global Warming Impacts

Even small temperature increases can transform entire ecosystems. Oceans, for example, are warming because they absorb most of the extra energy (in the form of heat) from the atmosphere. As of 2024 the average temperature of the upper layer of our oceans has risen by 0.67°F (0.33°C) since the 1970s. The less than 1-degree change in sea surface temperatures has caused major changes. Massive amounts of Arctic ice, ice sheets, and glaciers have melted. Scientists estimate that between 1994 and 2017, about 28 billion tons (25.4 billion t) of ice melted across the globe, and Arctic ice continues to melt at increasing rates. The melting glaciers add water to the sea, causing sea levels to rise. From 1920 to

2020, sea levels along the US coastline rose by 10 to 12 inches (25 to 30 cm). This alarms many people because the sea level had been about the same for the previous two thousand years. Even though these numbers are already out of the norm, scientists predict the sea will rise another 10 to 12 inches in just the next thirty years.

The warming oceans also cause acidification. The sea absorbs the excess heat and carbon dioxide, which changes the chemistry and acidity of the water. Ocean acidification refers to a change in ocean properties in which the ocean becomes more acidic and threatens any species that have

Billions of tons of glacial ice have melted since 1990, which has caused sea levels to rise.

bones (vertebrates) or shells in their bodies. Acidic waters weaken shells and bones and prevent species from reproducing. Acidic oceans also cause coral bleaching. Coral bleaching occurs when the corals become more fragile and stressed from acidic waters. This causes the small animals that live in corals, called polyps, to abandon the coral structures. The lively, bright corals become pale, as though they've been bleached. Ultimately, coral bleaching kills coral reef ecosystems that support thousands of other marine life species. But warmer and more acidic seas are only one piece of the climate change crisis puzzle.

Climate Change Impacts

Climate change can negatively impact food, water, and even air. It threatens both food supply and quality. This is because rising temperatures and shifting seasons harm crop production, soil quality, and water availability. Climate change also profoundly impacts marine life and causes fish populations to decrease or relocate, making it harder to fish and further contributing to food scarcity in many parts of the world.

There are also severe community consequences of climate change. Rising sea levels are especially concerning for coastal communities that already face floods and heavy storm surges. These rises threaten lives and livelihoods, causing increased stress in the populations who must move away from the coasts to stay safe. Additionally, the more severe weather patterns and global warming that result from climate change are threatening human health by increasing the spread of dangerous diseases such as malaria. Part of this is due to better breeding conditions for bugs, such as mosquitoes, that carry

Rising sea levels in Thailand's Bay of Bangkok, caused by coastal erosion and flooding that have worsened due to climate change, have prompted many families to relocate inland.

such diseases. As climates change or warm, bug populations can expand and spread to previously unaffected areas.

Climate change also worsens global poverty since vulnerable populations tend to feel its effects most. Countries and communities that lack resources are usually those that did not experience a mass industrial revolution and have larger low-income populations. So, they struggle to develop and acquire resources to prevent climate change and safeguard against or adapt to it.

Coastal communities and low-income regions are not alone. The whole world faces threats of climate change. Worldwide reports of temperature-related illnesses, spreading diseases, reduced air quality, extreme weather events and natural disasters, and food safety concerns are increasing, all because of climate change.

Taking Responsibility

All of humanity has no choice but to try to adapt to climate change and its consequences. Some people are more affected than others, and some people and organizations are more responsible for climate change than others. To take responsibility, countries that emit most of the greenhouse gases are coming together to help lower-income countries that impact the planet less adapt. For example, the Climate Risk and Early Warning Systems initiative funds projects in lower-income countries. It aims to save lives and livelihoods. Projects include providing early warning systems, including storm warning alarms such as cyclone sirens or radio data service alerts, to these countries and small islands. These solutions benefit the international community and the countries that are offering support. One benefit for everyone is that adaptation support is more helpful and less expensive than post-disaster humanitarian relief.

A rainfall and water level telemetry station equipped with an early flood warning system stands by the Sarawak River in Malaysia.

Climate change impacts are expensive for individuals, communities, and governments. All the impacts, including the damage to agriculture, buildings, properties, human health, and food supply, have financial costs. It is estimated that by 2050, climate change could cost the global economy more than $3 trillion. In 2023 it was estimated that the world is collectively spending more than 16 million dollars every hour to prevent and respond to climate change. There is no question that climate change is a crisis that demands our attention. That is why people and organizations are working tirelessly to protect the planet and limit the impact of this crisis.

Heavy damage near Fort Myers, Florida, caused by Category 5 Hurricane Ian in 2022, is an example of the billions of dollars climate change-related disasters cost every year.

CHAPTER SEVEN

The Future of Climate Change

For the first time on record, every day in 2023 had a temperature was more than 1.8°F (1°C) above the pre-industrial averages. Half of these days were 2.7°F (1.5°C) above the pre-industrial averages, and a couple of days skyrocketed to 3.6°F (2°C) above them. This made 2023 the warmest year on record so far. If people do not take action, climate models predict that by the turn of the century, humanity could be dealing with temperatures up to 9°F (5°C) above the pre-industrial averages. If we are already seeing such severe climate change impacts with a 1-degree change, imagine what 9°F (5°C) might mean for our planet.

Climate Models and Future Predictions

Climate scientists use modern technologies such as climate models to predict the future impacts of climate change. These predictions are crucial to understanding climate change and how we can prepare for its impacts. Climate scientists can adjust the factors in climate models and test different possibilities for the future. For example, scientists might adjust possible carbon dioxide emissions to see what the best- and worst-case outcomes could look like in the future. Scientists have used such climate models for decades, and studies confirm that many of their predictions have proven to be quite accurate. As the climate model predictions warn, Earth is on track to break life-threatening heat records if we do not lower our emission levels as soon as possible.

Global Organizations and Action

Governments and organizations around the globe are uniting to address climate change.

Among the largest and most well-known climate watch organizations is the IPCC. The IPCC uses science to study and understand climate change. Their studies help governments create and implement climate-related decisions and policies. The IPCC also participates in global efforts such as the UNFCCC, where countries gather to negotiate

Heat records are regularly being broken across the planet, and climate models warn that extreme heat will quickly get to life-threatening levels.

greenhouse gas emission goals and form agreements to address climate change.

Two of the most famous international agreements, or treaties, are the Paris Agreement and the Kyoto Protocol. The Kyoto Protocol was signed in 1997 and aims to reduce greenhouse gas emissions, especially in wealthy, industrialized countries. The Paris Agreement was signed in 2015 and aims to prevent rising temperatures as much as possible in the 196 countries that adopted it, making it the most significant climate agreement in history.

Climate Policy

Unlike climate treaties, which cannot be enforced, climate policies are laws, limitations, and standards enacted by governments that are designed to regulate carbon and greenhouse gas emissions. Climate policies come in many different forms. They include climate taxes, cap and trade methods, and clean energy standards. How do these climate policies work to address climate change?

Climate taxes have two forms: emission taxes and goods and services taxes. Companies that emit carbon and other fossil fuels must pay emissions taxes. Individual consumers must pay goods and services taxes when they purchase goods and services that use fossil fuels in their manufacturing.

Cap and trade methods limit greenhouse gas emissions and reward companies for using cleaner energy.

Clean energy standards require businesses to get a percentage of their electricity from renewable or clean (low or net zero emission) sources. Similarly, cars and transport systems set clean energy standards called fuel economy standards. This motivates car manufacturers to increase fuel efficiency, cut

Fuel economy standards are used to compel carmakers to increase fuel efficiency in their vehicles.

pollution, and incorporate more alternative fuels into both the manufacturing of vehicles and the vehicles themselves.

Although all these policies are a step in the right direction, they are only successful if they are put in place effectively. This means that part of these solutions' success depends on governments and large-scale corporations. The other part is where individuals come into the equation.

Individual Climate Action

As the biggest consumers of energy, large corporations are the primary contributors to climate change. While big companies are the biggest offenders, that doesn't let individuals off the hook. We all still have a role to play. After all, energy use is something everyone contributes to and can control. As English zoologist Dr. Jane Goodall famously says in speeches during public appearances, "What you do makes a difference, and you have to decide what kind of difference you want to make."

Individuals make choices every day about the food they eat, the energy use in their homes, how they get from place to place, the items they purchase, and their interaction with their communities. A few habits they should focus on include reducing food waste, recycling, carpooling and bike riding, and less energy use. To help, a 2023 study calculated the most effective actions individuals can take toward climate change. The study found that in addition to making more sustainable individual choices, demanding more accountability and action from governments and corporations is one of the most important actions you can take. In addition to lowering your personal carbon footprint, actions such as writing to harmful corporations or starting petitions that encourage companies to reduce their carbon footprint might be some of the most effective actions to take.

People can also pressure politicians, governments, and businesses to become more sustainable. In the United States, burning fossil fuels contributes to over 90 percent of all carbon emissions. In 2023 the four biggest sellers of fossil fuels, ExxonMobil, Shell, BP, and Chevron, reported $100 billion in combined profits, giving them little motivation to seriously regulate themselves. Boycotting companies with big carbon footprints and encouraging others to boycott them too is another action you can take.

Climate change action can also be as simple as interacting with your community. Climate scientists think that some of the most important actions in the fight against climate change include interacting with the public by putting together workshops and seminars, spreading awareness, and simply talking about climate change.

What Is Your Carbon Footprint?

The first step to lowering your carbon footprint is finding out what it is. Many environmental organizations offer free, easy-to-use carbon footprint calculators. To calculate your carbon footprint, enter information about your transportation habits, personal choices, home energy systems, and waste disposal methods. Once you see your footprint, keep in mind that these numbers are more like a baseline of the impacts of your habits. Variables can be adjusted to show how different habit changes affect your overall footprint. The best part? There are simple ways that you can lower it since even small actions make big differences.

Small Steps

Learning about climate change or other global crises can feel discouraging. But it's not too late to make a difference, and there have been encouraging signs of progress.

As it becomes more affordable, renewable energy is gradually replacing fossil fuels. Between 2008 and 2018, solar panels became 90 percent cheaper, and wind energy prices dropped by 70 percent. In 2024 it became cheaper to build a renewable energy plant than a new fossil fuel plant. Large companies and buildings are already transitioning, as some skyscrapers, such as the Empire State Building in New York City, run entirely on wind power. New carbon-capturing technologies are another potential solution for reducing carbon emissions. They remove carbon dioxide from the air and trap it. Once the CO_2 is captured, it is cooled and stored beneath

Earth's surface, causing little environmental impact. In Iceland, the first large-scale carbon capture plant was built in 2021 and is predicted to pull approximately 4,000 tons (3,629 t) of carbon dioxide out of the atmosphere each year. Although these technologies do have drawbacks and environmental effects of their own, they show promise for even better technology and progress in the future.

Another encouraging sign comes from the ocean. In 2016 climate change-fueled cyclones destroyed multiple coral reef ecosystems in Fiji. Scientists thought that the damage was too intense for the reefs to recover. Then, in 2020 the coral reefs demonstrated their resilience. They had not only recovered but were thriving as an abundant marine ecosystem.

Many countries are doing their part to stop climate change, too. Greenland, France, Spain, Denmark, Belize, and Ireland have banned drilling for fossil fuels and oil exploration (the search for fossil fuel deposits). Norway operates almost entirely with renewable energy sources, with 98 percent of its electricity coming from wind and hydroelectricity plants. The United Kingdom and the European Union have mandated that by 2035 all new car sales must be electric or renewable energy vehicles. In 2022 the United States created the Inflation Reduction Act, which allocated more than $360 billion toward global warming and climate change solutions.

These examples are just a few the many important steps being taken to slow or stop climate change. Humanity has a long road ahead to make significant changes, but there is hope that the climate crisis will improve. What is the best thing individuals can do to help humanity in its fight? Take any action, big or small! It all makes a difference.

CONCLUSION

The Only Option

From the food people eat to the clothes they choose to wear, climate shapes human life. Since the Industrial Revolutions, climate change has been a growing problem for humanity. In fact, it might be the biggest problem the world is facing. There is no other choice but immediate climate change action.

Understanding and adapting to the current impacts of climate change while also working to prevent future ones is essential. Without action, the planet is heading down a dangerous path. In North America alone, thousands of studies show climate change has resulted in devastating droughts, raging wildfires, rising temperatures, and extreme weather patterns. These changes threaten lives all around the globe, causing illness, ruining food supplies, and forcing people to relocate.

But everyone must be on board to combat this crisis. On a large scale, climate taxes, climate policies, and incentives for switching to renewable energy sources are all actions that can be taken toward achieving net zero emission goals. On an

Hitting the goal of net zero carbon emissions by 2050 will require large-scale individual and governmental action.

individual scale, people must evaluate their choices, work to lower their carbon footprints, and lead more sustainable lives.

So, how will you participate in the fight against climate change? Will you pressure your local government to adopt more sustainable policies? Will you educate your friends and family about carbon footprints? Will you make your home more sustainable by switching off lights and electricity when not in use? With enough people taking action and influencing the world around them, it is possible to indirectly help vulnerable people and communities, too. Small actions can prevent future generations from experiencing devastating impacts. Simple lifestyle changes, climate actions, and a determination to fight against climate change all make a difference.

GLOSSARY

adaptation: adjusting to change in a way that avoids harm or takes advantage of new opportunities

aerosol: particles or gases emitted into our atmosphere from either natural sources or human activity

albedo: the fraction or amount of light or radiation that is reflected off a surface

atmosphere: the mixture of gases that surround Earth

biodiversity: the variability of nature, environments, ecosystems, and living organisms; measured and compared between species, within species populations, and in ecosystems.

carbon dioxide (CO_2): a gas that is emitted when burning fossil fuels such as oil, gas, and coal; is a major contributor to global warming and climate change, owing to its potency, lifetime, and significant emissions.

carbon footprint: a measure of carbon dioxide emitted by an individual or a group based on regular activities and consumption that emit carbon

deforestation: the action of clearing a wide area of trees and natural habitat; the overall degradation of forests and natural environments

drought: a long period of abnormally dry conditions and less precipitation, leading to long-lasting effects on soil moisture

early warning system: a system that can generate appropriate and timely warnings to countries, communities, groups, and individuals threatened by hazardous impacts such as storms, cyclones, and floods

ecosystem: a biological community of living organisms and their interactions with each other and their specific environment

energy efficiency: the process of improving a method by reducing the amount of energy used to complete a task or make a product

fluorinated gas: any powerful greenhouse gas that comprises fluorine; human-made and are usually emitted by industrial processes.

food security: a situation where all humans have access to and can afford sufficient, safe, and nutritious food supplies that meet all dietary demands

fossil fuel emission: any carbon-based fuel such as oil, coal, and natural gases that is derived from the earth and emitted by human activities such as using electricity and transport

ice core: a cylinder of ice taken as a sample from a glacier or ice sheet to learn more about past climates

livelihood: a job, employment, or means that allows one to secure necessities, such as food and shelter

mitigation: an action that is taken to prevent or reduce the likelihood of future harm or loss

ocean acidification: a change in ocean properties over a long period owing to increased CO_2 absorbed by the seawater, leading to an increase in its acidity

ozone: an odorless and colorless gas that is made up of oxygen and occupies multiple layers of Earth's atmosphere

resilience: the capacity of different systems (environmental, human, and economic) to cope with hazards, events, or harmful impacts of global change, such as climate change

scenario: in climate science, a hypothetical future based on different emission rates and climate actions

solar radiation: energy emitted by the sun

sustainability: the act of maintaining or improving the state of the available natural resources with the aim of finding a balance and coexisting with nature without compromising it for future generations

vulnerable: the state and predisposition to be adversely affected or the lack of ability to avoid a hazard

SOURCE NOTES

6 "a change of . . . comparable time periods": *UN Climate Change Conferences UNFCCC*, International Organizations, 2002, web archive, https://www.loc.gov/item/lcwaN0017068/.

10 "Climate is what . . . what you get.": Caroline B. Le Row, *English as She Is Taught: Genuine Answers to Examination Questions in Our Public Schools* (New York: Cassell & Company Ltd, 1887), 934.

51 "What you do . . . want to make.": "What We Do," Jane Goodall Institute of Canada, accessed January 16, 2025, https://janegoodall.ca/what-we-do/.

SELECTED BIBLIOGRAPHY

Bandura, Albert, and Lynne Cherry. "Enlisting the Power of Youth for Climate Change." *American Psychologist* 75, no. 7 (October 2020): 945–951. https://doi.org/10.1037/amp0000512.

Brulle, Robert J. "Institutionalizing delay: Foundation funding and the creation of U.S. climate change counter-movement organizations." *Climatic Change* 122, no. 4 (February 2014): 681–694. https://doi.org/10.1007/s10584-013-1018-7.

Cheung, W., et al. "Large-scale redistribution of maximum fisheries catch potential in the global ocean under climate change." *Global Change Biology* 16, no. 1 (2009): 24-35. https://doi.org/10.1111/j.1365-2486.2009.01995.x.

Hansen, J., I. Fung, A. Lacis, D. Rind, S. Lebedeff, R. Ruedy, G. Russell, and P. Stone. "Global climate changes as forecast by Goddard Institute for Space Studies three-dimensional model." *J. Geophys. Res.* 93, no. D8 (August 1988): 9341–9364, doi:10.1029/JD093iD08p09341.

Loeb, Norman G., Gregory C. Johnson, Tyler J. Thorsen, John M. Lyman, Fred G. Rose, and Seiji Kato. "Satellite and ocean data reveal marked increase in Earth's heating rate." *Geophysical Research Letters* 48, no. 13 (2021). https://doi.org/10.1029/2021GL093047.

Mohajan, Haradhan. "Third Industrial Revolution Brings Global Development." *Journal of Social Sciences and Humanities* 7, no. 4 (December 2021): 239–251.

FURTHER INFORMATION

BOOKS

Jahren, Hope. *The Story of More: How We Got to Climate Change and Where to Go from Here*. New York: Delacorte Press, 2021.
This book, adapted from the original for young adults, analyzes a fifty-year timeline (from 1970 to 2020) considering climate change.

Mooney, Carla. *Climate Change*. Minneapolis: Abdo, 2024.
This book provides a comprehensive guide to basic climate change concepts for young people.

Schroeder, Rebecca. *Climate Change Effects: How Our World Is Affected*. Minneapolis: Twenty-First Century Books, 2026.
A comprehensive look at the impact of climate change on the earth.

Thomas, Keltie. *Rising Seas: Flooding, Climate Change and Our New World*. 2nd ed. Buffalo: Firefly Books, 2023.
This book analyzes climate change impacts by specifically delving into the effects of sea level rise.

Thunberg, Greta. *The Climate Book: The Facts and the Solutions*. London: Penguin Press, 2023.
This book is a call to action from a global climate icon.

WEBSITES

Chapter 7: The Earth's Energy Budget, Climate Feedbacks, and Climate Sensitivity
https://ipcc.ch/report/ar6/wg1/chapter/chapter-7
From the IPCC Sixth Assessment Report, this page dives into the science of energy budgets, climate feedback, and changes in emissions over time.

Climate
https://iucn.org/nature-2030/climate
The IUCN website provides a library of resources that help governments and individuals take climate action.

Climate Basics for Kids
https://www.c2es.org/content/climate-basics-for-kids/
This page will help you understand the science behind climate change, the impacts of a changing climate, and how you can help slow climate change and prepare for it.

High Tide Flooding
https://oceanservice.noaa.gov
NOAA hosts a wide variety of climate change and atmospheric research for the public, including these resources on high tide flooding.

What Is Climate Change?
https://climate.nasa.gov/what-is-climate-change
Learn more about climate change through NASA's scientific visualization resource.

INDEX

ABOUT THE AUTHOR

Kayla Andra grew up in Utah. As a teenager, she developed a love for traveling, volunteering abroad, and the ocean. Some of her endeavors include sea turtle conservation in Costa Rica, elephant conservation in Thailand, sea turtle rehabilitation in Thailand, white shark research in South Africa, and, most recently, working as a SCUBA divemaster in Indonesia. Kayla has a master's degree in marine biology and has studied the effects of climate change on small-scale fisheries. She continues to travel and freelance as a marine biologist, aiming to educate others about the sea and inspire them to find and follow their joy.

PHOTO ACKNOWLEDGMENTS

Bernhard Staehli/Shutterstock, cover; Brian Youchak/Shutterstock, p. 5; imageBROKER.com/Shutterstock, p. 7; wavebreakmedia/Shutterstock, p. 10; Jody Hinterleitner/Shutterstock, p. 12 ; Shutterstock AI Generator, p. 16; TR STOK/Shutterstock, p. 18; Wirestock Creators/Shutterstock, p. 20; Dmitr1ch/Shutterstock, p. 21; Maria Dryfhout;/Shutterstock, p. 23; Hamara/Shutterstock, p. 25; geni/Wikimedia Commons, p. 27; Everett Collection/Shutterstock, p. 28; piyaset/Shutterstock, p. 31; PreechaB/Shutterstock, p. 33; Rizar el pixel, p. 36; Thaweesak Thipphamon/Shutterstock, p. 37; Artsiom P/Shutterstock, p. 38; VectorMine/Shutterstock, p. 40; Steve Allen;/Shutterstock, p. 42; Mike Towers/Shutterstock, p. 44; BaniHasyim/Shutterstock, p. 45; Bilanol/Shutterstock, p. 46; reisezielinfo/Shutterstock, p. 48; michelmond/Shutterstock, p. 50; BOY ANTHONY/Shutterstock, p. 55.